The Dedicated Ex-Prisoner's Guide for Getting Through
The Halfway House

10 Things to Do
to Make Your Rehabilitative Stay
Short, Productive, & Profitable

The Dedicated Ex-Prisoner's Guide for Getting Through
The Halfway House

10 Things to Do to Make Your Rehabilitative Stay Short, Productive, & Profitable

Richard Bovan

This work is dedicated to all those

who have ever suffered

the indignity of imposed inequality.

1-5 Things to Do
to Make Your Rehabilitative Stay
Short, Productive, & Profitable

**6-10 Things to Do
to Make Your Rehabilitative Stay
Short, Productive, & Profitable**

**1-5 Things to Do
to Make Your Rehabilitative Stay
Short, Productive, & Profitable**

**6-10 Things to Do
to Make Your Rehabilitative Stay
Short, Productive, & Profitable**

"Building prisons to fight crime is like building cemeteries to fight disease."

- Jack Levin

It's Just a Term: "Halfway" Does Not Mean Half Free!

Wikipedia defines a halfway house as "an institution that allows people with physical, mental, and emotional disabilities, or those with criminal backgrounds, to learn (or relearn) the necessary skills to re-integrate into society and better support and care for themselves. As well as serving as a residence, halfway houses provide social, medical, psychiatric, educational, and other similar services. They are termed 'halfway houses' due to their being halfway between completely independent living on the one hand, and in-patient or correctional facilities on the other hand where residents are highly restricted in their behavior and freedoms." Though this definition of halfway houses is technically correct, many formerly incarcerated people tend to think that the term "halfway" is in reference to their freedom. They think, because of the word "halfway" and often due to being told such, that being in the halfway house means that they are half free and half incarcerated, and nothing could be further from the truth.

When it comes to the formerly incarcerated, being a resident of a halfway house does not constitute being half free. There is no such thing as being half free; either you're free, or not. The fact is, in the halfway house, you are *not* free. You are still wholly under the jurisdiction of the state or federal government's penal system, and it

behooves all pre-residents of halfway houses to fully comprehend that before actually becoming a resident, which is why the first chapter of this guide is about this very common but very dangerous misunderstanding.

This guide is strictly for formerly incarcerated persons, not residents of sober houses or mental institutions, which are also sometimes referred to as halfway houses. I spent a six-month term in the halfway house after serving a ten-year federal prison sentence, and I made it through without any hiccups or setbacks. However, while there, I observed many men and women getting sent back to prison, sometimes very quickly, oftentimes for small, very avoidable offenses and rule transgressions. So I decided to compose this guidebook because, more times than not, halfway house residencies are revoked for problems that stem from misunderstanding, or not having a clear understanding, of how to survive in that particular environment, with its unique sets of rules and expectations.

This guide is purposely short, simple, and to the point. No fluff information that isn't really needed; just the facts and the most-needed pointers that often go unsaid or that frequently need to be reiterated. What qualifies me to give the advice I give within this guide is not only my personal experience of being sent to and successfully making it through a halfway house, but also my extensive research that is based upon the experiences of many other people across the nation who either did or did not successfully complete their halfway house stay.

Conventional wisdom says that the smartest way to learn is by observing the successes and failures of others and the actions and mistakes that led up to them, and repeating the good actions that lead to success and not repeating the mistakes that lead to failures. Sounds simple, but many people still find it necessary to experience the failures for themselves before they learn what and what not to do. This guide is not for the type of people who insist upon learning things the hard way. It is for those who have intentions on sparing themselves some potential hardship by taking the smart route, and thus would see the value of keeping a small printed reminder around of what and what not to do in order to not only make it through the halfway house successfully, but also to make their time spent there as productive and profitable as possible. If followed, the advice given within these ten short chapters will help you do just that.

Don't Forget You're Still in Jail;
It's Their House, Not Yours

In prisons and jails, from the get-go it's pretty
much understood by all who is in charge there
(the correctional officers/guards and staff
administration). It's clearly understood what the
hierarchy is and where everyone stands, and
hardly ever is there any mix-up about that. This
partly stems from the fact that there are physical
barriers in place that prevent prisoners from
leaving and limits access to open society which,
along with other things, helps create an

enclosed cultural environment that is unique to being incarcerated. As a result, I've seen plenty of guys leave prison and come to the halfway house, and because of the absence of physical barriers and certain physical restrictions, begin to behave as if they are no longer inmates who are incarcerated — as if they now have the ability to pretty much do as they please. And because there are technically no "guards" at halfway houses, they begin not regarding the staff as being authority figures on par with prison staff. Which is a huge mistake, since halfway house staff members essentially have the power to immediately send you right back to jail or prison.

When coming into a halfway house, you should regard being transferred there no differently than you would regard being transferred to another prison or jail. Because in actuality, that is exactly what is being done. There's no difference. If you fall into the line of thinking that it is different, you are potentially setting yourself up for failure. Yes, there are different things available to you in the hallway house vs. prison or jail, but your status as an incarcerated person has not changed an iota. And if you don't keep that fact in mind and act accordingly, you'll quickly be reminded of it, albeit too late, when you're on the first thing smoking headed back to lockup to serve out the remainder of your time.

However, if you continue to maintain the restraint, mental composure, and physical discipline you had when you were behind the bars, fence, or wall, and regard the halfway house as a privilege and opportunity and not an entitlement, odds are you will fare well. You should keep the tangible reasons why you're there on the forefront of your mind at all times.

You are there for your own benefit, no other reason, but the only way to get what you need out of the experience is to maintain your presence in the halfway house and participate in the processes of criminal rehabilitation and reentry programming in conjunction with the benefit of an earlier release from incarceration.

While at the halfway house, do not take anything for granted and don't take anything personal. Nothing is owed to you and nothing there is personal; it's strictly business. Everyone entering a halfway house has to follow the exact same rules, for the most part. The goal is to successfully make it out of their "house" so that you can go to your own house or residence and really get to experience freedom, barring any restrictions from parole, probation, or supervised release that you may have. Most halfway houses have a policy that allows for most residents to eventually be put on home confinement after they've been there for a few months with no problems, which helps them get the ball rolling faster in terms of reacclimating themselves with family and free society. This too should be a goal, unless there are extenuating circumstances that make staying in the halfway house for a longer period of time a better prospect, which may indeed be the case for some individuals. But for the most part, the sooner you can get out of confinement the better, for both you and your family.

As long as you stay focused and always make it a point to remember that you are still wholly incarcerated while you're at the halfway house or under their supervision while on home confinement, you should be alright. That's the best (and only) start-out mindset to have if you are serious about successfully making it through.

If you do that, along with the other nine recommendations that are outlined within this guide, you will have a successful programming experience while at the halfway house and will hasten and qualify your return to free society, which is the goal.

#2

Learn the Rules of the House
and Follow Them to the Letter

In playing any game or sport, going to any school, or working on any job, there are always rules and regulations to learn in order to proceed properly with a realistic expectation of success. In these arenas of activity and many others, those who are the most abreast of the rules are typically the ones who end up winning or succeeding. Being a resident in a halfway house is no different in this regard. However, unlike a job or school or sport, in the halfway house, your *freedom* depends on you knowing and abiding by the rules, not just your salary or grades or your score in a game.

As previously stated, I've seen many people get to the halfway house and then quickly get sent back behind bars for breaking a small rule, sometimes without even being aware that they were breaking the rule. When this happens, it's hard not to have pity on the person getting sent back to lockup for doing something wrong that they didn't even know was wrong, but again, you're technically still incarcerated so there's nothing that you or anyone can do about it. I've seen people get sent back for missing curfew, missing appointments, not following a staff member's directive, having unauthorized items, etc., with little to no warning, regardless of whether it was an honest mistake or not. I've also seen people make such mistakes and get second or even third chances, but you do not want to rely upon anyone's good graces to keep you from getting sent back to prison. It's much better to rely on your own awareness and full compliance to keep you on positive ground.

At the halfway house, because you are expected to know the rules and be in full compliance with them at all times, ignorance of the rules cannot be used as an excuse. Just like ignorance of the law is never an excuse, as far as the legal system is concerned, for criminality in society. So, one of the best things you can do, even before you actually arrive at the halfway house, is familiarize yourself with the rules and expectations for residents at that particular facility. If you cannot find that information before you get there, you will certainly be afforded the info once you arrive. Usually you will receive a list of the rules and expectations

upon arrival, or they will be posted somewhere visible within the facility. Take the time to fully familiarize yourself with them, and maybe even memorize them if you can. Setting aside just ten or fifteen minutes of your day to do this can potentially save you from having a lot of problems and headaches in the future.

Once you are fully aware of what exactly is expected of you from that facility's managing staff, you can then begin to fully focus and plan out how your stay there will proceed. As long as you know what to do and not do and adhere to that, you are the only person that is in control of the outcome of your situation there. Barring something extraordinary occurring, there would then be no predictable reason why you wouldn't successfully make it through the halfway house. Therefore, as soon as you can, make sure to learn or even memorize the rules of the house.

And while you're at it, you should also memorize the general Five-P Rule of Success: **Proper Preparation Prevents Poor Performance!** This rule applies to pretty much everything in life. The fact is, proper preparation is a necessary step and a precursor to being successful at anything. Preparing is like looking at a map before a venture into unknown land, or hydrating yourself before undertaking a five-mile jog, or studying before a test - it only makes good sense to do so!

Those who don't prepare to win, are by default preparing to lose. So if you don't want to "lose" because you made a mistake or otherwise performed poorly while at the halfway house, apply the 5-P rule and fully prepare yourself by learning all the rules of the halfway house and then follow them to the letter. Those who don't will certainly have a much greater possibility of failure. The goal and purpose of preparation is to minimize the potential of failure down to the point of zero. At the end of the day, learning the rules and then following them is the simplest and smartest thing you can do, and there's no excuse or reason why anyone cannot or should not do that other than they do not take their own freedom seriously.

#3

Don't Associate with Troublemakers and Lackadaisical People

While in the halfway house, you will have the opportunity and choice to associate with many different people, most or all of whom were previously incarcerated just like yourself. You will likely observe that some of them, like yourself, will be taking the opportunity to be at the halfway house very serious, while others won't. For your own sake, you'll need to distinguish who does or does not have the same frame of mind as you as far as being determined to succeed while there and make the conscious decision to only befriend and/or associate with those who are positively like-minded. Your progression and survival at the halfway house literally depends on it.

No different than being inside jail or prison, in school or on a job, or just being in society period, whom you choose to associate with while in the halfway house is very important for many different reasons. In general, those who you choose to befriend or closely associate with says a lot about you and has a lot to do with who you are, who you're becoming, and how you think. **There's an old saying that goes, "show me your friends and I'll show you your future."** This is certainly true because, typically, troublemakers and criminal-minded people hang around with other troublemakers and criminal-minded people, while progressive, law-abiding people hang around other progressive, law-abiding people. And most troublemakers and criminal-minded people have a very predictable life forecast that usually involves incarceration and/or run-ins with authority figures. Therefore, if you are serious about not only successfully making it through the halfway house but also succeeding in life as a whole and not repeating the mistakes that previously led to your incarceration, you will make the decision to not associate with those who are not on that same page while in the halfway house.

More specifically, while in the halfway house, it behooves you to *only* closely deal with residents who are consciously working toward the same or similar goals as you. It's always good (and smart) to only fraternize and socialize with people who reinforce your best instincts and inclinations, and especially so when you're when under corrective supervision while attempting to undertake a positive personal transformation. If you do this, trust me, everyone will take notice, the halfway house staff included, and from that will come an expectation of success for you that is apparent even before you actually succeed, which is very important, because the more people that expect you to succeed, the more likely you will succeed. That's just how positive energy and momentum works. On the flip side of that, as far as negative energy goes, we all know that all it takes is one bad apple to spoil a whole bunch.

Just as importantly, you will also want and need to avoid those people who are not motivated to generate the daily hustler energy that is necessary to make positive things happen for themselves while in the halfway house. Lazy energy can be infectious and contagious, and you want to stay as far away from that as you can. Positive energy can also be infectious and contagious, and it may sometimes require boosts of external positive energy for you to not get discouraged by setbacks or the politics of the halfway house. Remember: You were sent there to basically do preparatory work on your life, your family, and your future, and if you have a lackadaisical mindset about it you most certainly will not accomplish all that you could and should accomplish while there.

Misery loves company and so does laziness, so you must always be on guard against that kind of energy in the halfway house. Understand that oftentimes, especially in circumstances like yours, it is the characteristic of laziness that creates

miserable situations. So stay vigilant, stay motivated, and never succumb to allowing lazy energy to penetrate and seep into your mindset, and a big part of doing that will be identifying and avoiding, like the plague, those who are clearly infected with it.

In short, troublemakers and lazy people have no place at a halfway house, and rarely make it through the rigors of rehabilitative programming successfully. The halfway house environment is not set up to be conducive to those two mentalities in particular, as it is supposed to be strictly for those who want and need that intermediary time to get their lives together and acclimate themselves to living a productive, crime-free life in mainstream society. Anyone with common sense knows that it is extremely unlikely that a troublemaking, lazy ex-con will survive for very long in society without returning to prison, or worse. Therefore, as someone who wants to have their best chance at obtaining and maintaining their freedom for the long-term, you'd best take heed to good advice and stay clear of these two mentalities while at the halfway house.

Get Up Early, Go to Bed Early

Upon arrival at the halfway house and completion of orientation, you will be expected to almost immediately start working on finding employment or, if you've somehow already secured a job, you will start leaving the halfway house every day for work. Many residents will also be scheduled for different types of programming, assignments, or classes, which will typically take place during daytime hours. Most of the halfway house staff is present during the daytime, especially during weekdays, and usually do routine inspectional walk-throughs and conduct observations of residents in the living areas while there, which are sometimes logged and used when evaluating residents' progress or the lack thereof. Therefore, in general, unless you are working the night or evening shift on your job, it is always best to rise and shine early and go to bed early while at the halfway house.

The fact is, you did not come to the halfway house to rest and sleep; you came there to work, and on many things. Primarily, you are there to work on the aspects of yourself that are not conducive to living a clean and law-abiding lifestyle. Forming productive habits is one of the things you should really be focused on, and managing your time maturely and wisely is one of those. Since halfway house stays are typically short, there is little time to waste while there.

Thus, spending your downtime sleeping or for nonproductive leisurely activity is not what you want to make a habit of doing. As a convicted felon or person with a criminal record, for whom opportunities are sparse in society, you will likely not be able to sustain yourself if you have those habits in the future, so it only makes good sense not to get into the practice of doing those things while you're at the halfway house.

We've all heard the cliché, "Nothing comes to a sleeper but a dream," and in the case of halfway house residents, this is potentially very true in the literal sense. In the real world, dreams don't come true during sleep; they come into fruition while you're awake and actively working towards them. In the real world, long sleepers don't usually make long money, as it is a universally accepted notion in most modern, job-based societies that "the early bird catches the worm." Whether you have a job or are self-employed, that saying is common cliché for a reason — **most movers and shakers of the world are up operating earlier in the day rather than later, and because of this, the daytime hours are when earning and learning opportunities are most apparent. That being the case, and your circumstances being as they are, these are certainly not the hours that you want to routinely spend sleeping or wasting time.** A much better and more productive practice is to go to bed early and get your rest at night and be energetic with each early morning rising, ready to commence putting that energy toward achieving your goals.

Speaking of energy, you should know that while money is a form of tangible currency that everyone knows about, depending on where you are and what you're doing, there are many other forms of currency, some of them being intangible. Currency, for the most part, is whatever can be used to achieve goals or obtain desired things at any given time. **In a halfway house setting, Energy, Effort, and Opportunity are three intangible forms of currency that can easily be converted into tangible currency, if managed correctly.** For many halfway house residents, these three "things" will be the first forms of currency they have in lieu of having actual money or tangible resources. If this is the case for you, then it is your responsibility to use that alternative currency in the best ways possible. You can do that by always having the right energy about yourself, being willing to put your best effort into whatever you do, and always being ready to take advantage of new opportunities that present themselves, or create your own opportunities.

If you make a habit of getting up early and going to bed early while in the halfway house, there is no downside to that; only an upside. You will not only potentially be avoiding certain kinds of trouble and problems that sometimes occur in halfway houses, you'll be forming a proper habit and honing a wholesome practice that undoubtedly will serve you well when working a job or running a business for yourself in the future. Just as importantly, you'll be getting enough rest, which is absolutely necessary to keep a clear and focused mind.

Find and Keep a Job

For some, finding and maintaining employment will be the most challenging component of their rehabilitative stay at the halfway house. For those who may have planned and prepared ahead of time or who have more resources at their disposal, finding and keeping a job won't be a problem. What is mostly true for everyone, though, is the fact that *keeping* a job can oftentimes be harder than getting a job while in a halfway house, because of some of the supervisory policies that halfway houses have that require them to make and maintain direct contact with your employer after you've been hired. Halfway houses typically must cross-reference whatever information you give them about your employer and the specifics of your employment directly with your employer. This is done in the interest of public safety, as you are technically still a criminally-convicted incarcerated person, and to legally ensure that your employer is fully aware of your status as such. While this policy and procedure can sometimes be a hindrance and a nuisance, it typically does not stop determined halfway house residents from finding and maintaining employment.

Finding a job while at the halfway house will be your first major priority. Reason being, most halfway houses give new residents a specific

amount of time to find a job, usually six weeks or less, and if residents fail to do so they get sent back to jail or prison. So you won't have time to waste or lollygag. If you already had certain job skills or experience before being incarcerated or have developed any skills while incarcerated, it would be wise to begin your job search by looking for employment within that particular field if possible. If you have acquired some knowledge, certification, or experience in carpentry, construction, electrical wiring, landscaping, food service, building maintenance, or any other form of skilled physical labor, and you take the time to study up on how to give a good job interview, you can likely find work fairly quickly within those fields.

Even if you have no specific training or skills in anything, jobs that requires hard physical labor are not as stringent when it comes to hiring ex-prisoners or ex-felons, whereas those occupations that are physically easier usually pay as much or more than hard-labor jobs but have more work history and educational requirements and engage in more personal background scrutiny during their hiring processes. It's not right and doesn't make much sense sometimes, but it's the way of the world. So, if push comes to shove and no gainful job opportunity presents itself, as a temporary halfway house resident, you should seek out a job within a field that most people in society don't want to be in and, once hired, keep it at least until your halfway house term is over and you can take the time to find something better. Since you are on a timeline to get a job when in the halfway house, you don't have much time to waste or spend on job hunts. At least initially, you may have to take whatever you can get.

Other than the short-time-to-find-a-job factor, I often suggest that most job-hunting halfway house residents focus on certain types of "undesirable" jobs (physical labor, low wage) while in the halfway house for this reason: Job discrimination for ex-prisoners, among the many other forms of social discrimination that we face, is very real and perhaps the most harmful of them all. It is the one form of general discrimination that most all ex-prisoners face that has the highest potential for holding us back in life by purposely and legally stifling our ability to proceed and progress in society, and for no good reason. It prevents us from getting jobs that we could otherwise get and likely succeed at. There really is no reason why a person who can, in theory, be hired to work on a construction site or in a fast food restaurant couldn't or shouldn't be eligible to also be hired to stock shelves at Wal-Mart or answer calls at a business's call center. (Wal-Mart does not hire ex-felons, and banks and businesses like Sprint and Amazon, who ironically employ people in foreign countries to do this same type of work, have policies that deny employment opportunities to Americans with criminal records.) Unfair and unneeded socially discriminatory policies like these need to be done away with, but will have to be worked around until they are.

Many jobs that will hire ex-prisoners can be found via word of mouth while in the halfway house. Since everyone there is required to have a job, you can inquire around for information that can lead to an interview or job from an employer who has already hired someone at the halfway house before, or who has employees there currently. Fast food restaurants are another source for quick employment. Really, any job or combination of jobs that you can get will do, as long as it is for full-time hours in terms of total weekly hours worked. Most halfway houses require that your employment be full-time, and some of them even have assistance programs set up to help residents obtain full-time employment if they cannot find it on their own.

While at the halfway house, it is important for you to remember that no matter your age or situation, there is no shame in working any job in order to maintain your freedom and take care of yourself and family. All work is important and though some jobs may pay better and get more respect than others, no form of work is actually more important than another. **Physical work may be hard, but look at it as exercise that you get paid to do.** I'm speaking from experience — that is the kind of self-talk I had with myself inside my own head when I was in the halfway house working a job as a building custodian. Whenever I had to work really hard and get all tired and sweaty, I reminded myself that some people exercise daily for free, or even pay gym fees and buy expensive equipment in order to do so. I remembered when I used to exercise every day in prison, which is considered a privilege in prison, and couldn't wait to do so. It's all in how you choose to look at it, while maintaining a bigger picture perspective. After all, having any job in free society is better than being forced to literally work for pennies in prison.

Therefore, do whatever you must do while in the halfway house to find and keep a job, no matter the job, and work that job to the best of your ability while you have it. Then, if you choose to and plan it out properly, you can put that all behind you once you have completed

your halfway house stay and move on to bigger and better things.

Create Realistic Goals
and Stay Focused on Them

Upon being released from jail or prison, it is tempting and easy for people to start imagining what all they will begin doing and achieving for themselves now that they're back in society. Many will imagine themselves doing "big" things that they never did before being incarcerated. Though there is absolutely nothing wrong with dreaming big and having grand ideas, it is also very important that newly released ex-prisoners maintain a sense of balance and stay conscious of the reality and limitations of their situation, especially in the beginning.

While some people in the halfway house may have head starts in getting themselves together because they have lots of familial and/or financial support at their disposal, most halfway house residents will likely not have such support at the ready and will need to begin rebuilding their lives from the ground up. Some residents will have served long prison sentences and will be partially or wholly unfamiliar with many of the current happenings and protocols of society. For those people especially, it is important to understand that pacing oneself and exercising humility will be very important ingredients in their progression and eventual success in whatever ventures they hope to embark upon.

For many ex-prisoners, it will also be tempting to try to do as much as possible as fast as possible and make up for the time they lost due to their incarceration. Moving too fast, trying to do too much too fast, is a common mistake that many ex-prisoners make. Though you may seemingly be moving in a positive direction, moving too fast too soon can sometimes bring about some of the same negative effects as other more clearly recognizable bad habits that you're being warned against in this guide. The same can be said for having unrealistic goals. **Do not unnecessarily set yourself up for disappointments and downfalls by putting too much pressure on yourself too soon.**

For the determined ex-prisoner, being patient, taking your time, and having a great deal of humility will help take you a long way and greatly increase the chances of your eventual long-

lasting success. Part of the purpose and mandate of halfway houses is to allot residents some crucial time to focus and get themselves together before being one hundred percent on their own. This is why they initially provide room and board, meals, rehabilitative programs, counseling, and other forms of guidance and assistance. Take advantage of all of that while at the halfway house and take time to think about and prepare for the long-term as well as the short-term.

Some residents rush to relieve themselves of what they consider to be the "burdens" of the halfway house — the authority figures, the rules, the curfews, the constraints and lack of total freedom — but then often find themselves one day wishing they had used that time more wisely while they were there. Don't be one of those people who chooses to always focus on the bad within any given situation. **Coming back into society to start over after being absent for a significant amount of time is no joke and should never be taken too lightly.** To the contrary, it should be regarded very seriously and managed with the utmost care and caution, because your freedom, your happiness, the well-being of your family, and your life are all literally at stake. Don't compromise all of that by being unfocused, unrealistic, rushed, or negative.

Create a multitude of realistic short-term goals and stay focused on them in order to bring about the realization of positive and progressive big-picture, long-term goals. Take one cautious step at a time, and always be honest with yourself and think about the realistic and likely consequences and outcomes of whatever it is you plan to do, not just the outcomes you wish for or want to occur. This will ensure that, at the very least, you are always fully aware of, and therefore in control of, all the eventual outcomes of your actions.

In some ways, a formerly criminal-minded person coming into free society after being incarcerated for significant time is like a newborn baby coming into the world — if they're serious about not ever being incarcerated again, then like the newborn baby they must learn to do everything anew. And just like a newborn, for the newly released ex-prisoner, there is a stage or period of time where assistance in doing that is most helpful and most needed, and that's in the very beginning. In the beginning for the baby, there is a time for crawling, then a time for walking; a time for baby food, then a time for solid food; a time for diapers, then a time for independent bathroom usage; a time for baby talk, then a time for actually talking. And as we all know, there is a learning process involved in all of those things, as no baby ever walks before they crawl or talks before being taught a language. Since the average ex-prisoner halfway house resident also has to learn or relearn the basics of societal survival, then the halfway house is exactly where this particular learning activity should begin taking place. Halfway houses are tailor-made for just that purpose and any time spent there should strictly be used as such. Because once you are discharged from the halfway house, you are pretty much one hundred percent on your own, and that time will come soon enough; it is *not* good to be in too much of a rush for it.

Plus, you don't want to have to keep restarting your efforts or expend extra energy and resources correcting mistakes that were made from rushing or not taking your time, which almost always happens. Instead, while in the halfway house, focus not so much on getting things done fast, but on being realistic and getting things done *right*. Reason being, when it's all said and done, only the things that are realistically executed and done right succeed and last.

Create or Solidify
Your Family Situation

Leaving the halfway house upon completion of the requirements of your residency is almost like being released from brick-and-bars prison or jail all over again, and is usually regarded as such by many residents. After being discharged, most residents will go and live with family or friends while others will immediately need to procure independent housing for themselves. For those residents that do not have supportive family situations that allow for you to have somewhere to live upon release, it is best to stay at the halfway house for as long as possible in order to save money and take more time to create and solidify your living situation. (Most halfway houses will not force such residents to accept home confinement even if they are eligible for it, precisely for the forestated reasons.) But for those residents who do have family or friends that are willing to open their doors for you and assist in your transition from the halfway house back into the community, it is best to begin cultivating and solidifying your relationships with them before being released.

Your family and friends are a big part of your life and thus will be a big part of your rehabilitation, recovery, and reentry into society. It behooves dedicated ex-prisoners to make sure that the friends and family that they choose to fraternize with are conducive to living a law-abiding lifestyle and not enablers for any forms of negativity. Family and friends have a way of either helping to keep their loved ones out of trouble, or helping to keep them in trouble. Birds of a feather usually *do* flock together, so if you are serious about your continued freedom and progression you should always ensure that you only deal with people who will enable and encourage you to do the right things at all times.

If you do have family and friends, let them know what your intentions are for when you are fully released from custody and continually show them with consistent words and actions that you are extremely serious about what you say. They will be watching you closely, whether you know it or not, to see if you in fact are serious about what you say your intentions are. Take care not to cause your supportive loved ones and friends to disbelieve you or lose confidence in you by not following through with your stated intentions, as family and friends will typically only be as serious about your progression as you've show yourself to be. They will take their cues directly from you. If you are not serious about yourself, they likely won't be either. If you are not consistently focused on the right things for yourself, they likely won't be either, and if they are, not for long. It is up to you to define and solidify exactly what it is that you expect and want from your close family and friends as well as from yourself, and they will most certainly follow your lead on that.

For most family and friends of newly released formerly incarcerated people, them being released from incarceration usually comes with either an expectation of an overhaul or change of some sort on the part of their released loved ones, or just more of the same old same old. They usually expect to see some changes in personality, mentality, and physicality, and will instinctively be on the lookout for such. If they do not see or feel positive energy and positive change coming from you, it will be that much harder and less convenient for them to reciprocate that positivity back to you. And trust me, you will need that positive reciprocation from those closest to you. So, with your family and friends, be sure to properly set the stage for yourself with them even before your full release from incarceration and the halfway house by staying consistent and focused on your freedom, success, and new healthy, law-abiding lifestyle.

Ex-prisoners coming into a halfway house who do not already have close and supportive family and friends should be mindful of the benefits and value of a "supporting cast" and be looking to create a positive social circle for themselves at some point. **There is a well-known old cliché that says "No Man is an Island," meaning, every person needs input from other people in order to be what they want to be, do what they want to do, or to get where they want to go.** It's true that no one truly fails in life all by themselves, and just as true that no one can truly succeed in life all by themselves, and if they feel that they can, then whatever they do achieve certainly won't measure up to what they could have achieved had they had support from other people. So do not look to be an "island" on your quest for productivity and positivity as an ex-prisoner — look to create and solidify a familial and associative situation for yourself that involves strong like-minded people that will be an asset to your healthy progression, and you to theirs.

When one lives only for oneself, you tend to not be as mindful of how your actions affect the lives of others. But when you are not only living for yourself but also for those around you that you love and care about, better decisions tend to be made. Always remember that, along with another observation that also is worthy of note: Statistics show that most ex-prisoners that have healthy personal relationships or who are happily married, have the lowest recidivism rates; they do not repeatedly return to prison. I encourage all dedicated ex-prisoners to research this stat for yourselves, and then ponder upon how such a fact may or may not affect or apply to your own personal situation.

Save Your Money!

In the halfway house, there will be lots of things that you are required to do or not do, and there will be supervision and limitations on many aspects of your life and activities. However, there will be other aspects of your life and activities that will be left totally under your control. While some halfway houses do offer resident-specific compulsory financial planning and savings plans for various reasons, for the most part, how your money gets managed while you're in the halfway house will be up to you.

Generally speaking, everyone in the halfway house will need to try to save money for when they are fully discharged from their residency, but it typically will not be an easy task for many. There are expenses associated with your halfway house stay — halfway houses typically require residents to pay 25% of their gross earnings directly to the halfway house — plus other personal living expenses that are or may be associated with your transportation, clothing, food/snacks, medical, child support and/or other family expenses, fines, and other obligations. (While in a halfway house, residents who have healthcare insurance must use it to cover their own medical expenses, while those who don't have it can use Medicaid and Federal Financial Participation to cover these services.)

Because most ex-prisoner halfway house participants have felony criminal records and thus do not readily qualify for employment at higher wage, higher qualification-oriented jobs, the typical salary or wage received by most will not be such that a whole lot of money saving can realistically be done. However, the more money you can manage to save, the more prepared you will be upon your eventual discharge from the halfway house. This may mean that you have to eliminate or limit certain personal expenditures like extra clothing or other recreational spending while there, in order to be more financially prepared later on. It may mean that you have to work more hours or more than one job. Whatever it means for you, it would be best for you to begin doing it as early as possible upon arrival at the halfway house so as to begin saving the most money possible in preparation for your post-halfway house future.

For ex-prisoners that are dedicated to succeeding and never being incarcerated again, discipline is the name of the game, and success, not just survival, is the ultimate goal. Reaching success is usually a proverbial marathon, not a sprint, and nobody runs a marathon with hopes of winning without preparing/sacrificing extensively beforehand. So, in the halfway house, when it comes to your money, it may be prudent to attempt to save every dime possible and spend no money that doesn't absolutely have to be spent. Being shrewd is usually the smartest way to go when it comes to money anyway, and especially so when you are a convicted criminal with limited resources who's nevertheless serious about building a better future for yourself and your family.

If you didn't have substantial money saved prior to your incarceration but you saved shrewdly while at the halfway house, when you get released from the halfway house, trust me, you will need and have use for every dollar that you've managed to save up. So, don't get caught up in buying stuff that you want but don't really need or trying to keep up with the Joneses while in the halfway house; if you play your cards right, you will eventually get the chance to obtain those wants and more. Until then, it's best to keep it simple and be frugal.

Set a weekly or bi-weekly budget for yourself and stick to it. Think about getting a savings account and always keep up with your expenses and financial obligations, minimizing them whenever possible. Always be looking to find ways to increase your earnings and decrease your expenses, which increases your savings, until you get to a point where you're truly comfortable and stable. It will take time — if you do it right, it's *supposed* to take time. Just like Rome wasn't built in a day, your success will not come fast or without substantial work and planning being conducted on your part. **Financial planning is a big part of financial success. For halfway house residents, that financial success can be activated and realized with just three actions: Earn as much as you can, plan as much as you can, and save as much as you can.**

#9

Use Downtime
to Develop Entrepreneurial Ideas

For ex-prisoners with felony criminal records who want to maximize their quality of life in spite of being legally disqualified from attaining gainful employment, entrepreneurship is the way to go. What is considered "gainful" employment is most often associated with college graduates, and implies higher wage work in a white-collar or skilled blue-collar position. Debt level, financial commitments and other monthly expenses also affect the extent to which one is "gainfully" employed. Having non-gainful employment means that although you have a job, which is always a good thing regardless, it's a J.O.B (Just Over Broke) and you likely will not be able to fulfill many of your extracurricular wishes or maintain a lifestyle that requires more disposable income. Therefore, the best way to be able to fulfill your long-term dreams and goals and provide better opportunities and amenities for yourself and family is to, at some point, develop sound entrepreneurial ideas and then venture into gainful self-employment.

And here's the best part about doing that: **In the entrepreneurial/business ownership world, criminal records don't really matter.** When applying for a typical job in society, background checks are done, drug tests are conducted, your credit is often checked, and all kinds of questions are asked about your history, affiliations, and abilities. Personal scrutinization goes hand in hand with job attainment in today's world. And with a consistently highly saturated job market, gainful employment attainment standards will likely only get more extensive in the upcoming future. But if you are the owner of a company or business, none of these things apply to you and you can own and operate your business with the same level of non-scrutiny and autonomy that non-felon business owners enjoy.

In the halfway house, you'll have times when you have nothing to do while at the facility or at home on home confinement, and these are the times when you should be mapping out your entrepreneurial course of action. In doing that, you must determine, realistically, what all it will take in order to bring your plan into fruition. There are plenty of aspects to creating and running a business that require pre-planning and focus as well as tangible resources, and it would be unwise and wasteful to not begin putting it all together, even if it's just in your mind, as soon as it's possible to do so. Find a quiet spot in the halfway house to sit and contemplate on it and maybe even write down your thoughts. **If you're really serious about becoming successful, you'll want to use every bit of time you have while you're in the halfway house to better yourself, and not waste time or take for granted that there will be other times to get things done.** Trust me, you'll have more spare time while at the halfway house than you'll have once you're out and on your own, so use it to do some of the mental legwork that needs to go into your future entrepreneurial venture(s).

When developing your entrepreneurial ideas, it is best if they involve an occupation, product, or service that you are already familiar with or would enjoy doing, because being an entrepreneur requires consistency and dedication on a level that is higher than what is typically involved when one is working for someone else on a job. So, it's best to be extremely knowledgeable and as familiar as possible with what you plan on being involved with. Thus, it only makes good sense for you to use your downtime to do extra research and begin honing and preparing yourself in whatever ways needed in order to proceed and succeed in your upcoming entrepreneurial efforts.

If you happen to be one of those people who is able to get a job that you are satisfied with and/or you have certain job skills that allow you to readily get decent-paying jobs and you aren't interested in being an entrepreneur, that is fine as well. Everybody cannot be an entrepreneur, nor does everybody want to be. Some ex-felons do manage to get good jobs and maintain careers, as there are exceptions to pretty much every rule, but realistically speaking, we all know that this is not the case for the overwhelming majority of ex-felons. At the end of the day, it's up to you to make a way for yourself and to choose the best way to do that, for yourself. For some, it will be working a job; for others, it will be entrepreneurship and business ownership.

My personal recommendation is that, if possible, ex-felons should gear their minds toward eventually owning and operating their own businesses, for all the forestated reasons. However, in making your living, as long as it is what *you* want and you're happy with it and you can comfortably sustain your household, it makes perfect sense to choose whichever path you feel best works for you. Whichever path you choose, job or entrepreneurship, if you work hard and make smart decisions, as an ex-felon with all the odds against you, you're a success story either way. Again, as long as you have an acceptable level of happiness and satisfaction when it comes to your occupation, that's all that really matters.

#10

Prepare for Freedom:
Preset Healthy Habits and Keep the
Unhealthy Past in Your Rear View

The functional definition of insanity is doing the same thing over and over again while expecting different results — the obvious flip side to that is, in order to get different results from something, you must do something different. Once you are released from halfway house supervision, you will have the opportunity to forge a completely new pathway, to plant a new seed, if you will, to a new life that bears new

and good fruit and not more of the bad fruit
that was produced by your past actions and
habits. You will have the opportunity to create
and live a renewed, refreshed and redirected life
that is totally disconnected from anything and
anybody that would not be a healthy and
positive influence on you. In preparing for long-
term freedom and success while in the halfway
house and out, you must concentrate on
forming and practicing these new healthy habits
consistently, so as to ensure that you never
revert back to the old unhealthy habits that did
not serve you well in the past.

Practice makes perfect, and to be good at
anything, practice is a requirement. But practice
requires time to get it right. Notwithstanding any
preparatory actions you may have taken while
you were still locked behind bars away from
society, the perfect time to begin really putting

new social habits into action is when you're at the halfway house because there you're actually in society for much of the time. You can make plans of what to do while you're incarcerated behind bars; when at the halfway house and while on probation, parole, or supervised release, it's time to literally put those plans into daily practice.

The key to putting them into practice consistently is to first fully commit to discarding all the old negative stuff — the unhealthy persons, places and things of the past along with your unhealthy thoughts and actions that are linked to them. In doing that, you're making room in your psychological rolodex for new habits and new persons, places and things to come into. Your habitual capacity is like a closet; there is finite room there and you cannot put in too many new things without first discarding some of the old stuff. **You should never try to commit to a new habitual mentality without first committing to fully abandoning your old one.** So, make it a point to permanently discard the old and negative habits first, then replace them with the new and positive habits. Mixing old bad habits with new good ones is a recipe for disaster and almost always leads to a relapse of costly bad behavior that stems from instinctively reverting back to those old bad habits at certain points, and especially when under pressure. Bad habits have to be totally discarded and then replaced — if not, they'll have the chance to hang around dormant within your psyche and then pop up when it's least convenient and potentially cost you big-time, and you don't want or need that if you're seriously trying to turn your life around for good.

Once you've committed to getting rid of those bad habits and formulating and keeping only the new good ones, I promise you, many things in your life will go a lot smoother for you! You'll have better results in just about everything that you set out to do. More opportunities and more good people will gravitate towards you. Healthy habits create healthy outcomes and brings healthy energy into your life, and that is what you need and should want almost more than anything. Healthy energy also helps engender a healthy attitude, and as they say, your attitude often determines your altitude in life. **Bad habits, negative people, bad places, and a bad attitude are all the main ingredients for a recipe for disaster for ex-felons, so be sure to stay clear of all four.**

For some people, discarding all those bad habits may be a strenuous process, but for most,

I'm convinced that it doesn't have to be much of
a process — like the Nike mantra says, you can
"Just Do It!" By that I mean, all it takes is you
making the decision to do it, being deadly
serious about it, and remaining consistent and
disciplined in your efforts towards that from day
to day. That's it! If you do that, you've got a very
important part of your rehabilitation and
successful reentry down pat and there is no way
that you will fail. And I'm not just talking this; I've
lived it! I've done it myself, and so have many
others that I know.

My first book, *The Dedicated Ex-Prisoner's
Guide to Life & Success on the Outside: 10 Rules
for Making It in Society After Doing Time*, is a
bestseller because it details exactly what ex-
prisoners and ex-felons need to do to not only
survive, but succeed in society. I encourage you
to read it and apply all the recommendations

and principles that are offered within it as well.

From my perspective, getting out of a prison, a

jail, or even a halfway house is indeed like being

born again with a chance to perform a do-over,

irrespective of the all the obstacles facing ex-

prisoners and ex-felons. It's a chance that

thousands of prisoners will never get because

they have already squandered it by one means

or another, and it is best that you look at it that

way instead of focusing on the negative aspects

of it. Have a "this glass is half full" and not a "this

glass is half empty" kind of mentality, as it'll take

you much further than dwelling on the negative.

**Think positive, say positive, and do positive, and
your outcomes will be positive more times than
not.** If you prepare well, put and keep the

unhealthy past in your rear view, and execute,

then freedom, as well as success, *will* be yours. I

guarantee it!

Other Recommended Readings
for Halfway Houses and Rehabilitation Centers

The Dedicated Ex-Prisoner's Guide
to Life & Success on the Outside:
10 Rules for Making It in Society After Doing Time
by Richard Bovan

Getting Out & Staying Out:
A Black Man's Guide to Success After Prison
by Demico Boothe

Making Good:
How Ex-Convicts Reform & Rebuild Their Lives
by Shadd Maruna

Prisoners Once Removed: The Impact of Incarceration and
Reentry on Children, Families, and Communities
by Jeremy Travis, Michelle Waul

But They All Come Back:
Facing the Challenges of Prisoner Reentry
by Jeremy Travis

Other Recommended Readings
for Halfway Houses and Rehabilitation Centers

The Master Plan:
My Journey from Life in Prison to a Life of Purpose
by Chris Wilson

Criminal Reform: Prisoner Reentry into the Community
by Quintan B. Mallenhoff

Beyond Bars: Rejoining Society After Prison
by Jeffrey Ian Ross, Stephen C. Richards

Barriers to Reentry? The Labor Market for Released
Prisoners in Post-Industrial America
by Shawn Bushway, Michael A. Stoll,
David F. Weiman

Complete Survival Guide
for Newly Released Prisoner and Family: Life After Prison
by Serge Mezheritsky